Talking Hands

COLORS AND SHAPES

COLORES Y FORMAS

WRITTEN BY KATHLEEN PETELINSEK AND E. RUSSELL PRIMM
ILLUSTRATED BY KATHLEEN PETELINSEK

A SPECIAL THANKS TO OUR ADVISERS: AS A MEMBER OF A DEAF FAMILY THAT SPANS FOUR
GENERATIONS, KIM BIANCO MAJERI LIVES, WORKS, AND PLAYS AMONGST THE DEAF COMMUNITY.

CARMINE L. VOZZOLO IS AN EDUCATOR OF CHILDREN WHO ARE
DEAF AND HARD OF HEARING, AS WELL AS THEIR FAMILIES.

The Child's World

Published in the United States of America by The Child's World®
PO Box 326, Chanhassen, MN 55317-0326
800-599-READ
www.childsworld.com

Photo Credits: Brand X Pictures/Burke/Triolo Productions: 5, 19;
Photodisc: 14; Photodisc/C Squared Studios: 8, 17; Stockbyte:
cover (left and right), 1 (left and right), 11, 20-21, 23.

The Child's World®: Mary Berendes, Publishing Director

Editorial Directions, Inc.: E. Russell Primm, Editorial Director; Katie Marsico
and Elizabeth K. Martin, Associate Editors; Kathleen Petelinsek and E. Russell
Primm, Photo Researchers

The Design Lab: Kathleen Petelinsek, design, and page production; Kari
Thornborough, production assistant

LIBRARY OF CONGRESS CATALOGING-IN-PUBLICATION DATA
Petelinsek, Kathleen.
  Colors and shapes = Colores y formas / by Kathleen Petelinsek and E. Russell
Primm ; content advisers, Carmine L. Vozzolo and Kim Bianco Majeri.
    p. cm. — (Talking hands)
  Summary: Provides illustrations of American Sign Language signs and Spanish
and English text for various colors and shapes.
  English, Spanish, and American Sign Language.
  ISBN 1-59296-019-7 (lib. bdg. : alk. paper) 1. American Sign Language—
Vocabulary—Juvenile literature. 2. Spanish language—Vocabulary—Juvenile liter-
ature. 3. Colors—Juvenile literature. 4. Shapes—Juvenile literature. [1. American
Sign Language—Vocabulary. 2. Spanish language—Vocabulary. 3. Polyglot
materials. 4. Color. 5. Shape.] I. Title: Colores y formas. II. Primm, E. Russell,
1958- III. Title.
  HV2476.P473 2004
  419'.7—dc22   2003018691

NOTE TO PARENTS AND EDUCATORS:

The understanding of any language begins with the acquisition of vocabulary, whether the language is spoken or manual. The books in the Talking Hands series provide readers, both young and old, with a first introduction to basic American Sign Language signs. Combining close photo cues and simple, but detailed, line illustration, children and adults alike can begin the process of learning American Sign Language. In addition to the English word and sign for that word, we have included the Spanish word. The addition of the Spanish word is a wonderful way to allow children to see multiple ways (English, Spanish, signed) to say the same word. This is also beneficial for Spanish-speaking families to learn the sign even though they may not know the English word for that object.

Let these books be an introduction to the world of American Sign Language. Most languages have regional dialects and multiple ways of expressing the same thought. This is also true for sign language. We have attempted to use the most common version of the signs for the words in this series. As with any language, the best way to learn is to be taught in person by a frequent user. It is our hope that this series will pique your interest in sign language.

Red
Rojo

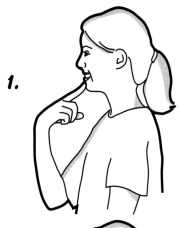

1.

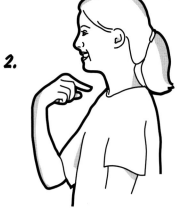

2.

Triangle
Triángulo

1.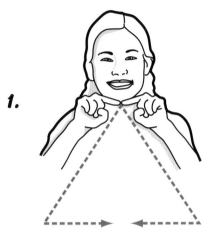

2.

Watermelon
Sandía

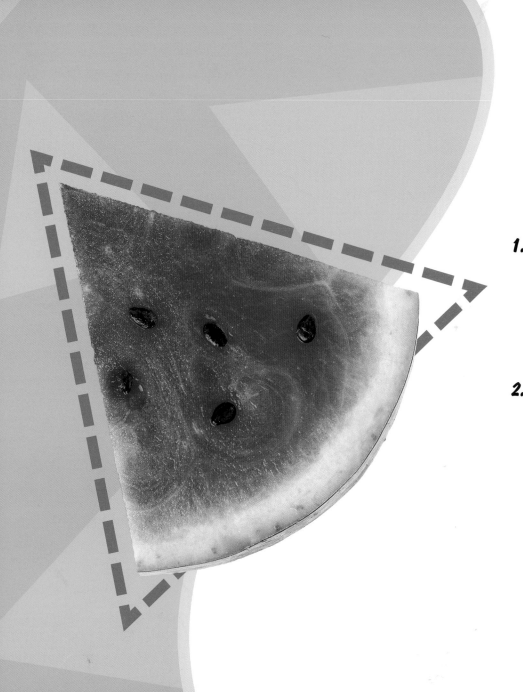

1.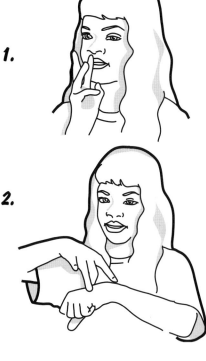

2.

**For step 2, motion
thumping a melon.
Para el paso 2, haga el gesto
de golpear un melón.**

Orange
Anaranjado

1.

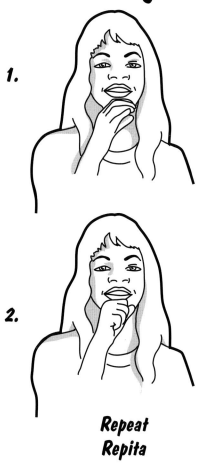

2.

Repeat
Repita

Circle
Círculo

1.

Basketball
Pelota de
Baloncesto

1.

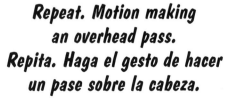

Repeat. Motion making
an overhead pass.
Repita. Haga el gesto de hacer
un pase sobre la cabeza.

Yellow
Amarillo

1.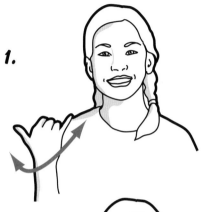

2.

Repeat
Repita

Rectangle
Rectángulo

1.

2.

Cup
Taza

1.

2.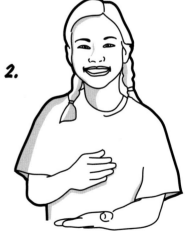

Repeat
Repita

11

White
Blanco

1.

2.

Oval
Óvalo

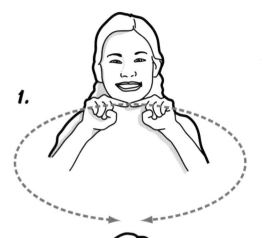

1.

2.

Egg
Huevo

1.

2.

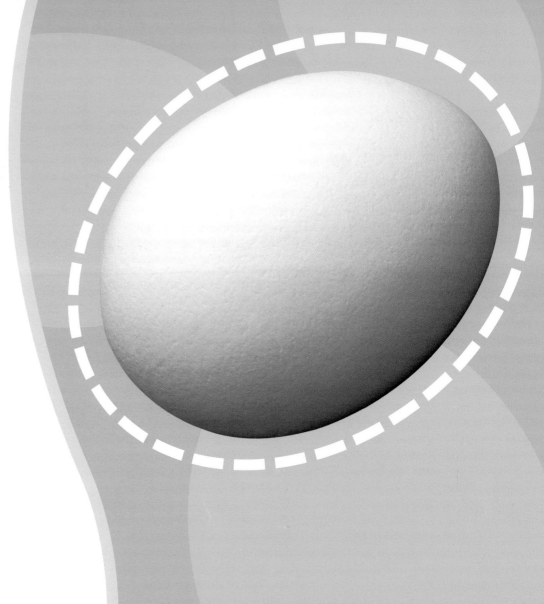

Black
Negro

1.

2.

Square
Cuadrado

1.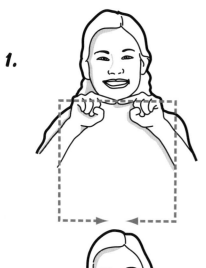

2.

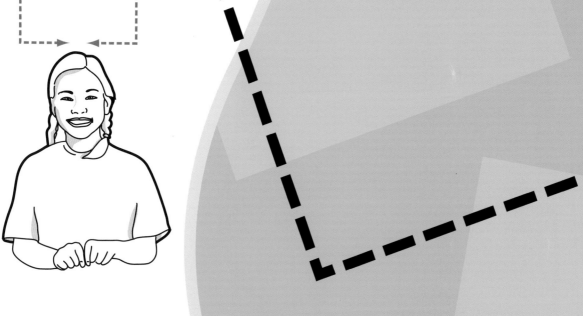

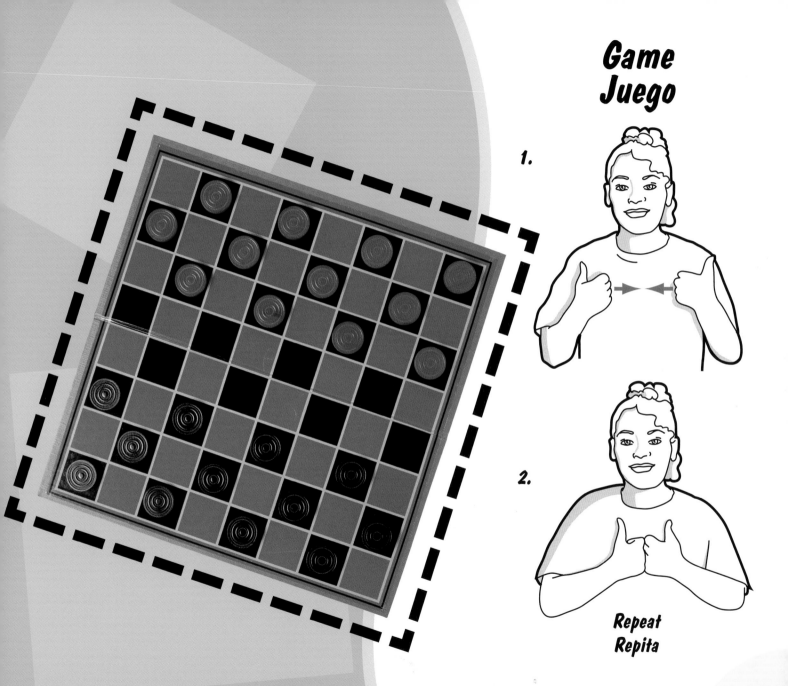

Game
Juego

1.

2.

Repeat
Repita

17

Purple
Morado

1.

Repeat (Note: The fingers are
positioned the same as the
sign for the letter P.)
Repita (Nota: Los dedos se
posicionan de la misma manera
que la señal para la letra P.)

Grapes
Uvas

1.

2.

**Small tapping motion
on back of hand
Pequeño golpe en la parte
trasera de la mano**

19

Blue
Azul

1.

2.

Repeat
Repita

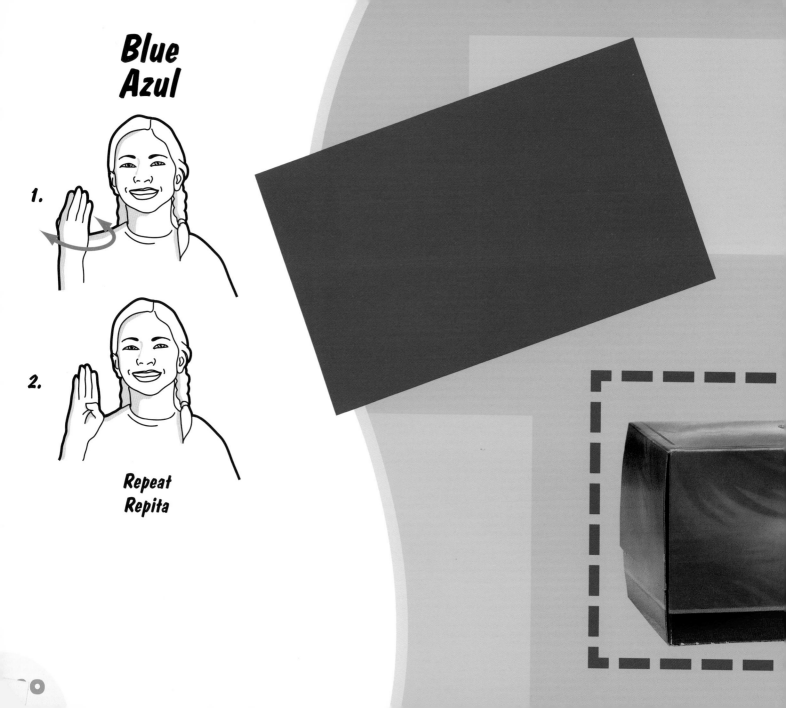

Tissue
Pañuelo de papel

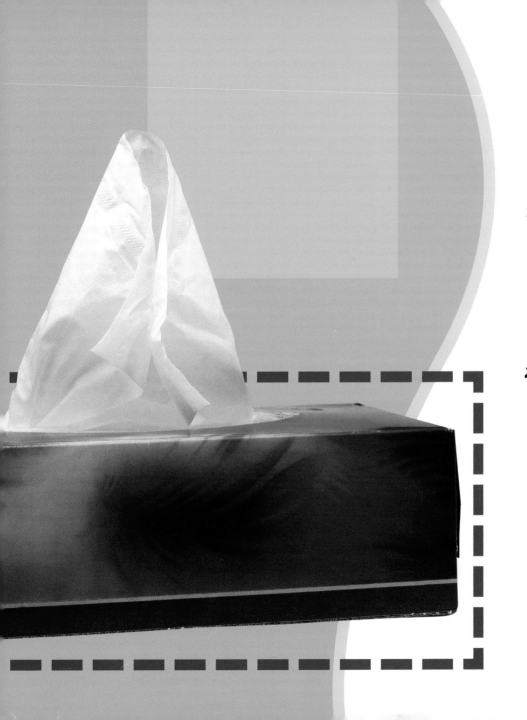

1.

2.

Repeat
Repita

Green
Verde

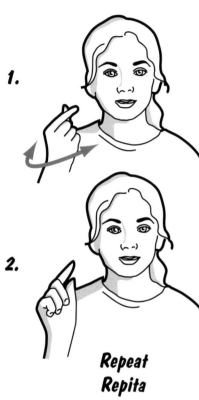

1.

2.

Repeat
Repita

Bottle
Botella

1.

2.

23

A B C D E F

G H I J K

L M N O P

Q R S T U

V W X Y Z

A SPECIAL THANK-YOU

to our models from the Program for Children Who Are Deaf and Hard of Hearing at the Alexander Graham Bell Elementary School in Chicago, Illinois:

Aroosa is in third grade in Milwaukee and loves reading, shopping, and playing with her sister Aamna. Aroosa's favorite color is red.

Carla is in fourth grade and enjoys art, as well as all kinds of sports.

Deandre likes playing football and watching NFL games on television. He also looks forward to going to the movies with his family.

Destiny enjoys music and dancing. She especially likes learning new things and spends much of her time practicing her cursive handwriting.

Xiomara loves fashion, clothes, and jewelry. She also enjoys music and dancing. Xiomara's favorite animal is the cat.